Bibliographic information published by the German National Library:

The German National Library lists this publication in the National Bibliography;
detailed bibliographic data are available on the Internet at http://dnb.dnb.de .

Imprint:

Copyright © 2008 GRIN Verlag, Open Publishing GmbH
Print and binding: Books on Demand GmbH, Norderstedt Germany
ISBN: 9783640663279

This book at GRIN:

http://www.grin.com/en/e-book/153918/political-economy-of-the-global-media-
business-why-corporate-interests

Sebastian Plappert

Political Economy of the global media business: Why corporate interests shape the news

GRIN Publishing

GRIN - Your knowledge has value

Since its foundation in 1998, GRIN has specialized in publishing academic texts by students, college teachers and other academics as e-book and printed book. The website www.grin.com is an ideal platform for presenting term papers, final papers, scientific essays, dissertations and specialist books.

Visit us on the internet:

http://www.grin.com/

http://www.facebook.com/grincom

http://www.twitter.com/grin_com

ICOM 816 Communication & Political Economy

Sebastian Plappert

Political Economy of the global media business:
Why corporate interests shape the news.

In traditional liberal thinking the press operates as "the people's watchdog" who critically evaluates political decisions (Hudson 1999). Thereby, the media has to be organised by private citizens or organisations independent of government censorship and control (Pasley 2001). As long as government intervention is prevented, the free press will guarantee the free flow of information and ideas (Martin 2001). Since democracies build upon "popular sovereignty" the citizens as the ultimate decision makers have to rely on public access to information in order to make sound political choices (Meiklejohn 1960, pp. 8-28). Following conventional wisdom, the government and the private media are by nature in conflict with one another, and therefore, public interest is served best by letting the balancing forces of the market regulate the media system (Lichtenberg 1987). As a consequence "the communication system has emerged as a central area for profit making in modern capitalist societies" (McChesney & Schiller 2003, p. 1).

Much has been written about media corporations growing in size and reach, but since theoretical framework and findings correlate with each other, there is a wide range of research from various perspectives (Wasko 2005). Whereas an array of authors perceives these developments as unavoidable for the media operating in an era of globalisation (Bauman 2000; Stiglitz 2002; Gledhill, 2004), others point to the dangers for democracy and call for public interference (Schiller 1981; Parenti 1993; Barnouw & Gitlin 1998; Bagdikian 2000; McChesney 2000a, 2000b, 2001; Herman and Chomsky 2002). Closely connected to critical and Marxian theory (Murdock & Golding 1979), a political economy approach has to consider "the social relations, particularly the power relations, that mutually constitute the production, distribution, and consumption of resources" (Mosco 1996, p. 25). Accordingly, this paper will briefly trace recent developments in the media industry, before examining the role of the state and neo-liberal ideology in shaping the global communication system. After analysing the effects of media concentration, special focus will be put on the concept of commodification in the media industry and the notion of cultural hegemony and dependency of media. Thereby, it will be argued that elitist corporate interests shape the news content in order to guarantee a profit friendly political environment.

Media concentration

During the past decades, the global communication system has undergone a variety of dramatic changes, shifting power to commercial interests. Technological improvements in digital communications created an increasingly global market for corporations looking for investment (Schiller 1999). Thereby, predominantly western companies engaged themselves in "conglomeration and transnationalization" through corporate takeovers, mergers and acquisitions of unprecedented scale (Jin 2007, p. 185). These ongoing processes of vertical and horizontal integration fostered the emergence of huge media conglomerates (Jamison 1998; Schiller 2001). Vertical integration, the acquisition of related businesses in the process of profit generating (Gomery 1986), enables corporations to effectively produce, distribute and broadcast its products under one roof and, therefore, minimise transaction costs (Stigler 1964). In other words, a corporation owning production companies and distribution outlets, as well as TV stations and movie theatre chains, simultaneously provides itself with its own supply and demand. Horizontal integration, on the other hand, aims at obtaining a greater share of the market by acquiring companies in the same field of business in order to maximise profit through price control (Gomery 1986). Hence, only a hand full of globally operating corporations remained, with the majority of them based in the US (Jin 2007, p. 191). Since "many of the largest media firms have some of the same major shareholders, own portions of one another or have interlocking boards of directors" (McChesney & Schiller 2003, p. 12), eventually, "the global media system is fundamentally noncompetitive in any meaningful economic sense of the term" (McChesney 1998, p. 5). Whereas "the ownership structure of the news industry purportedly aligns the news media's coverage of the economy with the overall business interests of the corporate community" (Kollmeyer 2004, p. 435), the "oligopolistic control of much of the world communication market by a few giant corporations" renders it not only practically impossible for newcomers to penetrate the market (Jin 2007, p. 148), but, in consequence, enables these firms to "behave as if a monopoly were operating" (Gomery 1989, p. 50). Lacking any effective competition, the intertwined ownership structure of the media industry cultivates the shaping of media content according to underlying corporate interests.

Neo-liberal ideology and the role of the state
The rise of this global commercial media system is closely linked to the assertion of neo-liberal capitalism as the dominant theory of economics. Being "significant beneficiaries" of the current global structure, the media giants have a particular interest in supporting the perpetuation of neo-liberal capitalism (McChesney & Schiller 2003, p. 13). Since the unregulated free market as the fairest and most effective way of wealth distribution is the essential precondition for a prospering democratic society (Harvey 2005), there is no need for the public to interfere in the current organisation of media ownership (Touraine 2001). Thereby, both consumerism and corporate concentration are depicted as natural (Bauman 2000), inevitable consequences of globalisation (Cowling & Tomlinson, 2005; Sklair, 2002). However, since globalisation, and thereby neo-liberal ideology, "was restored by [US] military force and national policy, it was not a 'natural' state of affairs" (Hirst & Thompson 2002, p. 249). Economic neo-liberalism strongly relies on governments forming a global regime that "defines and guarantees, through international treaties with constitutional effect, the global and domestic rights of capital" and enterprises (Panitch 1994, p. 64). Hence, there is no reason for Hirst and Thompson (2002, p. 248) to assume that all the processes linked to globalisation "have an inherent dynamic that prevails

over all countervailing forces". Neo-liberalism is not a dogmatic consequence of globalisation, and despite the general perception of globalisation representing "an unstoppable historical force in the face of which politics is helpless" (Scott 1997, pp. 1-2), it remains reversible (Williamson 1998, p. 70), always dependent on governmental backing (Scholte 1997, p. 442). Moreover, as an instrument of an overarching ideology of free market capitalism, neo-liberalism "is grounded in the [ever-increasing] power of multinational corporations arguing for free trade by means of removing political and governmental rules and regulations that may inhibit the movements of goods, services and capital across borders" (Nafstad et al. 2007, p. 316). In summary; "the centerpiece of neoliberal policies is invariably a call for commercial communication markets to be deregulated" (McChesney 2001, p. 2). Obviously, governments played key roles in the communication sector because political intervention was necessary to implement something resembling a free-market regime in the communication sector (Schiller 1999, Mosco & Schiller 2003). Since government policies are often shaped by the interests of the corporate sector (Monbiot 2000), the behaviour of the regulators largely reflects the interests of the regulated (Mercer 1995). Accordingly, "the global media system is the direct result of the sort of 'neoliberal' deregulatory [...] agreements that have helped to form global markets" in the first place (McChesney 1998, p. 2). Following Galtung's (1979) theory of structural imperialism, the harmony of interests between business and government is not restricted by state boundaries. On the contrary, favorable conditions for corporations to maximise profit abroad are in the interests of "periphery" state elites, as well as of the "center nation" as a unit (Galtung 1979, pp. 83-85). Thereby, "private media and governments are [...] seen as partners, [...] serving those sitting atop of the social pyramid" in each society (McChesney & Schiller 2003, p. 4). Given the "political rewards [... of] attracting and retaining transnational investment, governments are often compelled to accommodate favourable [...] measures", such as privatisation and ownership deregulation (Cowling & Tomlinson, 2005, p. 44). Consequently, the global media cartel avoids covering controversial issues about property or socio-political relations, and focuses on neo-liberal values and interests, in order to consolidate their position (McChesney 2004). As Nafstad et al. (2007, p. 316) conclude, "this variant of modern capitalist ideology creates values that concentrate wealth and power in the hands of few, thereby legitimising social inequalities". Since global media corporations belong to these profiting few, legitimation is simultaneously strategy and reason for them to shape media content benevolent towards the status quo.

Commodification

Moreover, the inherent logic of neo-liberal capitalism naturally leads to corporate bias in the news. Following McChesney (2001, p. 8), "the best way to understand how closely the global commercial media system is linked to the neoliberal global capitalist economy is to consider the role of advertising". Being the "the necessary transmission belt for businesses to market their wares across the world (McChesney 2004, p. 12), the commercial media companies are the main profiteers. Whereas competition decreased due to acquisitions, global market share for each media corporation remarkably increased, in percentage as well as in absolute terms (Jamison 1998), therefore, "competitive behavior is [...] diverted away from price [and content] towards [...] advertising competition" (Cowling & Tomlinson, 2005). As "the mass media are first and foremost industrial and commercial organizations which produce and contribute commodities", it will provide content that generates maximum revenue (Murdock & Golding 1974, pp. 205-206). Since "advertising" from globally operating corporations[1] "represents the primary source of income" for all media companies (Kollmeyer 2004, p. 435), it is argued that this practice predetermines an anti-critical bias towards corporate interests (Bagdikian 2000, pp. 105-73; Herman 1999, pp. 13-28; Herman & Chomsky 2002, pp. 13-8). Hence, advertising is a characteristic of corporate power and in turn sustains and enhances it (Klein 2000).

Accordingly, audiences are addressed as consumers, not as citizens, which translates into the "commercial media, whether directly related to news information or encompassing news and entertainment, deflect[ing] attention away from information and concerns important for an informed citizenry and instead favour[ing] content that supports the ubiquity of commercialism" (Huntemann 2005, p. 27). However, not only media content is reduced to a commodity, so is the audience (Smythe 1977). Following Smythe's concept, media content is produced in order to attract a "commodity audience", which in turn is sold to advertisers (Wasko 2005, p. 29). Thereby, "some parts of the commodity audience are more valuable than others" (Meehan 2007, p. 164). Since advertisers predominantly target affluent upper and upper-middle classes beneficially integrated into the economic system, media content will be designed at primarily this valuable group of customers (Gitlin 1983). Whereas "relatively sophisticated business news" (McChesney 1998, p. 9) are "pitched to the business class and suited to its needs and prejudices", media content "reserved for the masses tends to be the sort of drivel" (McChesney & Schiller 2003, p. 14), that is either completely depoliticised entertainment or pieces of corporate PR. According to the propaganda model (Herman & Chomsky 2002), with "the dominant media [...] firmly imbedded in the market system" (Herman 1996, p. 117), corporate "PR is welcomed by media owners, as it provides, in effect, a subsidy for them by providing" free content, and, therefore raising the profit margin (McChesney 2000b, p. 8). "The conflation of news production and entertainment [for example ...], has resulted [...] in news information geared toward supporting the commercial interests of entertainment companies" (Huntemann 2005, p. 26). Furthermore, the propaganda model states "that the mainstream media, as elite institutions, commonly frame news and allow debate only within the parameters of elite [business] interests" (Herman 1996, p. 121). "Lacking any necessary conspiratorial intent and acting in their own economic self-interest, media conglomerates exist simply to make money" (McChesney & Schiller 2003, p. 14). Hence, they resort to cost efficient sources and align their content with advertiser needs, which in turn further promotes the dominating economic framework.

---

[1] Due to the process of concentration, some of them are partially owned by huge media conglomerates themselves.

Cultural hegemony

Additionally, these large media conglomerates promote media content favorable to elitist business interests because they are themselves ideologically part of the elite. As Gramsci (1931) argued, elites maintain their socio-economic privileges through cultural hegemony over society. Thereby, "major institutions of civil society, by promoting ideas and cultural norms supportive of the existing socioeconomic order, help generate widespread public consent for the structural inequality inherent within capitalist societies" (Kollmeyer 2004, p. 434). Instead of providing the means to publicly debate important issues (Habermas 1991), the mass media portrays the economy in a way that affirms the existing economic system, by interpreting events from a pro-capitalist perspective (GUMG 1976, 1980). Strongly influenced "by the commercial needs of the organizations that control the means of communication" (Huntemann 2005, p. 30), "culture itself is a manifestation of ideological interests" (Altheide 1984, p. 477). Therefore, cultural hegemony is seen as a self-perpetuating concept (Sallach 1974; Hall 1979), that leads the media to focus on the culturally "dominant audience and ignore minority cultures" or alternative views (Gomery 1989, p. 55). It "advances corporate interests and values, and disintegrates or ignores that which cannot be incorporated into its mission" (McChesney & Schiller 2003, p. 13). Whereas "corporate media culture tends to promote a deep and profound de pollicization" (McChesney & Schiller 2003, pp. 14-15), media companies themselves maintain strong ties with business policy groups, social clubs, and political parties (Akhavan-Majid & Wolf 1991), through interlocking associations and personnel (Dreier 1982; Witcover 1990). "Since prominent journalists and editors are tangential members of the [...] elite themselves" (Kollmeyer 2004, p. 437), major media corporations have no incentive to question the desirability of the prevailing economic system (Croteau 1998). Not only are journalists socialised into professional norms and work routines which are build upon the dominant ideology (Gans 1979; Hall 1979; Reese 1990), but media companies predominantly rely on corporate or official sources (Croteau 1998). As "the mass media are drawn into a symbiotic relationship with powerful sources of information by economic necessity and reciprocity of interest" (Herman & Chomsky 2002, p. 14), media content mirrors the dominant perception about the economic structure. Moreover, "the same logic of domination which infuses audience messages about their own social and cultural affairs also extends to an audience's view of the world" (Altheide 1984, p. 479). The concept of cultural hegemony depicts that large media conglomerates "share common viewpoints with corporate [and political] leaders about many important economic issues, and that these common viewpoints ultimately influence the manner in which the news media cover the economy" (Kollmeyer 2004, p. 437).

Corporate public sphere

In the face of a given empirically documented bias towards an uncritical coverage of economics beyond the neo-liberal framework (Gamson et al. 1992; Parenti 1993; Bagdikian 2000; Kollmeyer 2004), the political economy approach is an appropriate and useful tool to expose the underlying causalities leading media conglomerates to shape news content. The compelling logic of neo-liberal capitalism combined with the oligopolic media dominance achieved through government assistance enables business elites "to defend their interests and [further] propagate a mythology to protect their privileged role in society" (McChesney & Schiller 2003, p. 1). The currant media oligopoly actively advances its interest of profit-maximisation, which presupposes a favourable business environment. Additionally, the self propelling effect of neo-liberal ideology enhances the hegemonic dominance of corporate media concentration. Consequently, as idealistic Habermas' (1974) concept of public sphere may be, the current system of global communications seems more like a corporate public sphere, where the public is replaced with an elite pushing system compliant ideas to be sold by an at least ideological media monopoly.

Bibliography

Akhavan-Majid, Roya, and Wolf, Gary, 1991. 'American Mass Media and the Myth of the Libertarianism: Towards an 'Elite Power Group' Theory'. *Critical Studies in Mass Communication*, Vol. 8, pp. 39-151.

Altheide David 1984. 'Media Hegemony: A Failure of Perspective'. *The Public Opinion Quarterly*, Vol. 48, No. 2, pp. 476-490.

Bagdikian, Ben, 2000. *The Media Monopoly*, 6th ed. Boston: Beacon Press.

Barnouw, Erik, and Gitlin, Todd (eds.), 1998. *Conglomerates and the Media*. New York: New Press.

Bauman, Zygmunt, 2000. *Liquid modernity*. Cambridge: Polity Press.

Cowling, Keith, and Tomlinson, Philip, 2005. 'Globalisation and corporate power'. *Contributions to Political Economy*, Vol. 24, No. 1, pp. 33-54.

Croteau, David, 1998. 'Examining the 'Liberal Media' Claim: Journalists' views on Politics, Economic Policy and Media Coverage'. *EXTRA!*, 01 July 1998.Retrieved 17 April, 2008
http://fair.org/reports/journalist- survey.html

Dreier, Peter, 1982. 'The Position of the Press in the U.S. Power Structure'. Social Problems, Vol. 29, pp. 298-310.

Gamson, William; Croteau, David; Hoynes, William, and Sasson, Theodore, 1992. 'Media Images and the Social Construction of Reality'. *Annual Review of Sociology*, Vol.8, pp.373-393.

Gans, Herbert, 1979. *Deciding What's News*. New York: Vintage Books.,

Gitlin, Todd, 1987. *Inside Prime Time*. New York: Phanteon.

Gledhill, John, 2004. 'Neoliberalism'. In: Nugent, D. & Vincent, J. (eds.), *A companion to the Anthropology of politics*, Malden: Blackwell, pp. 332-348.

Gomery, Douglas, 1986. 'Vertical Integration, Horizontal Regulation: The Growth of Rupert Murdoch's US Media Empire'. *Screen*, Vol. 27, No. 4, pp. 78-87.

Gomery, Douglas, 1989. 'Media Economics: Terms of Analysis'. *Critical Studies in Mass Communication*, Vol. 6, pp. 43-60.

Gramsci, Antonio, 1932. *Selections from the Prison Notebooks*. [1971] London: New Left Books.

GUMG [Glasgow University Media Group] (ed.), 1976. *Bad News*. London: Routledge & Kegan Paul.

GUMG [Glasgow University Media Group] (ed.), 1980. *More Bad News*. London: Routledge & Kegan Paul.

Habermas, Jürgen, 1974. 'The public sphere'. New German Critique, Vol. 1, No. 3, pp. 49-55.

Habermas, Jürgen, 1991. *The Structural Transformation of the Public Sphere: An Inquiry into a Category of Bourgeois Society*. Cambridge: MIT Press.

Hall, Stuart, 1979. 'Culture, the Media and the 'ideological' effect'. In Curran, James, et al. (eds.), *Mass Communication and Society*. Beverly Hills: Sage, pp. 315-45.

Harvey, David, 2005. *A brief history of neoliberalism*. Oxford: Oxford University Press.

Herman, Edward, 1996. 'The propaganda model revisited'. *Monthly Review*, Vol. 48, No. 3, pp. 115-129.

Herman, Edward, 1999. *The Myth of the Liberal Media: An Edward Herman Reader*. New York: Peter Lang Publishing.

Herman, Edward, and Chomsky, Noam, 2002. *Manufacturing Consent: A Political Economy of the Mass Media*. 2nd ed. New York: Pantheon.

Hirst, Paul and Thompson, Grahame, 2002. 'The Future of Globalization' *Cooperation & Conflict*, Vol. 37, No. 3, pp. 247-266.

Hudson, Mark, 1999. 'Understanding Information Media in the Age of Neoliberalism: The Contributions of Herbert Schiller'. *Progressive Libarian* [online], No. 16. Retrieved 11. May 2008.
http://libr.org/pl/16_Hudson.html

Huntemann, Nina, 2005. *Policy and Culture in the Digital Age: A Cultural Policy Analysis of the US Commercial Radio Industry*. Amherst: University of Massachusetts Press.

Jamison, Mark, 1998. 'Emerging patterns in global telecommunications alliances and mergers'. *Industrial and Corporate Change*, Vol. 7, No. 4, pp. 695-713.

Jin, Dal Yong, 2007. 'Transformation of the World Television System under Neoliberal Globalization, 1983 to 2003'. *Television & New Media*, Vol. 8, No. 3, pp. 179-196.

Klein, Naomi 2000. *No Logo*. London: Flamingo.

Kollmeyer, Christopher, 2004.'Corporate Interests: How the News Media Portray the Economy'. *Social Problems*, Vol. 51, No. 3, pp. 432-452.

Lichtenberg, Judith, 1987. 'Foundations and Limits of Freedom of the Press'. *Philosophy and Public Affairs*, Vol. 16, No. 4, pp. 329-355.

Martin, Robert, 2001. *The Free and Open Press: The Founding of American Democratic Press Liberty*. New York: New York University Press.

McChesney, Robert, 1998. 'The Political Economy of Global Media'. *Media and Development*, Vol. 45, No. 4, pp. 1-10.

McChesney, Robert, 2000a. 'Journalism, Democracy, … and Class Struggle'. *Monthly Review*, Vol. 52, No. 6, pp. 1-15.

McChesney, Robert, 2000b. *Rich Media, Poor Democracy: Communication Politics in Dubious Times*. New York: New Press.

McChesney, Robert, 2001. 'Global Media, Neoliberalism, and Imperialism'. *Monthly Review*, Vol. 52, No. 10, pp. 1-19.

McChesney, Robert, 2004. 'The Political Economy of International Communications'. In Thomas, P. and Zaharom Nain (eds.). *Who owns the Media: Global Tends and Local Resistances*. Penang: Southbound, pp. 3-22.

McChesney, Robert, and, Schiller, Dan, 2003. 'The Political Economy of International Communications Foundations for the Emerging Global Debate about Media Ownership and Regulation'. *United Nations Research Institute for Social Development* [online], Technology, Business and Society Programme Paper No. 11, pp. 1-33. Retrieved 11. May 2008.
http://www.unrisd.org/80256B3C005BCCF9/httpNetITFrame?ReadForm&parentunid=C9DCBA6C7DB78C2AC1256BDF0049A7 74&parentdoctype=paper&netitpath=http://www.unrisd.org/unpublished_/tbs_/chesney/content.htm

Meehan, Eileen, 2007. 'Understanding how the popular becomes popular: The role of political economy in the study of popular communication'. *Popular Communication*, Vol. 5, No. 3, pp. 161-170.

Meiklejohn, Alexander, 1960. *Political Freedom*. New York: Harper.

Mercer, Helen, 1995. *Constructing a Competitive Order: The Hidden History of British Antitrust Policies*. Cambridge: Polity Press.

Monbiot, George, 2000. *Captive State: The Corporate Takeover of Britain*. London: MacMillan.

Mosco, Vincent, 1996. *The Political Economy of Communication: Rethinking and Renewing*. London: Sage.

Mosco, Vincent, and Schiller, Dan (eds.) 2001. *Continental Order? Integrating North America for Cyber-Capitalism*. Lanham: Rowman & Littlefield.

Murdock, Graham, and Golding, Peter, 1974. 'For a Political Economy of Mass Communications'. In: Miliband, Ralph and Saville, John (eds), *Socialist Register*, London: Merlin Press, pp. 205-234.

Murdock, Graham, and Golding, Peter, 1979. 'Capitalism, Communication and Class Relations'. In: Curran, James; Gurevitch, Michael, and Woollacott, Janet (eds), *Mass Communication and Society*. Beverly Hills: Sage Publications, pp. 12-43.

Nafstad, Hilde; Blakar, Rolv; Carlquist, Erik; Phelps, Joshua, and Rand-Hendriksen, Kim 2007. 'Ideology and Power: The Influence of Current Neo-liberalism in Society'. *Journal of Community & Applied Social Psy*chology, Vol.17, pp. 313-327.

Panitch, Leo, 1994. 'Globalisation and the state' In: Miliband, R. & Panitch, L. (eds.), *Socialist Register*, London: Merlin Press, pp. 60-93.

Parenti, Michael, 1993. *Inventing Reality: The Politics of the Mass Media*. 2nd ed. New York: St. Martin's Press.

Pasley, Jeffrey, 2001. *The Tyranny of Printers.: Newspaper Politics in the Early American Republic*, Charlottesville: University Press of Virginia.

Reese, Stephen, 1990. 'The News Paradigm and the Ideology of Objectivity: A Socialist at The Wall Street Journal'. *Critical Studies in Mass Communication*, Vol. 7, pp. 390-409.

Sallach, David, 1974. 'Class domination and ideological hegemony'. *The Sociological Quarterly*, Vol. 15, pp. 38-50.

Schiller, Dan, 1981. *Objectivity and the News*. Philadelphia: University of Pennsylvania Press.

Schiller, Dan, 1999. *Digital Capitalism: Networking the Global Market System*. Cambridge: MIT Press.

Schiller, Dan, 2001. 'World Communication in Today's Age of Capital'. *Emergences*, Vol. 11, No. 1, pp. 51–68.

Scholte, Jan, 1997. 'Global Capitalism and the State' *International Affairs*, Vol. 73, No. 3, pp. 427-452.

Scott, Allan, 1997. 'Introduction: Globalization: Social Progress or Political Rhetoric'. In: Scott, Allan (ed.), *The Limits of Globalization: Cases and Arguments*, London: Routledge, pp. 1-22.

Sklair, Leslie, 2002. *Globalization: Capitalism and its alternatives*. Oxford: Oxford University Press.

Smythe, Dallas, 1977. 'Communications: Blindspot of western Marxism'. Canadian Journal of Political and Social Theory, Vol. 1, No. 3, pp. 1-27.

Stigler, George, 1964. 'A theory of oligopoly'. *Journal of Political Economy*, Vol. 72, pp. 44-61.

Stiglitz, Joseph, 2002. *Globalization and its discontents*. New York: W.W. Norton.

Touraine, Alain, 2001. *Beyond neoliberalism*. Cambridge: Polity Press.

Wasko Janet, 2005. 'Studying the political economy of media and information'. *Comunicação e Sociedade*, Vol. 7, pp. 25-48.

Williamson, Jeffrey, 1998. 'Globalization, labour markets and policy backlash in the past' *Journal of Economic Perspectives*, Vol. 12, No. 4, pp. 51-72.

Witcover, Jules, 1990. 'Revolving-Door Journalists'. *Washington Journalism Review*, Vol. 12, No. 3, 33-38.

YOUR KNOWLEDGE HAS VALUE

- We will publish your bachelor's and master's thesis, essays and papers

- Your own eBook and book - sold worldwide in all relevant shops

- Earn money with each sale

Upload your text at www.GRIN.com and publish for free